A STUDY GUIDE FOR SMALL GROUPS
BASED ON THE BEST-SELLING BOOK

Gary Smalley & John Trent, Ph.D.

NAVPRESS
A MINISTRY OF THE NAVIGATORS
P.O. BOX 35001, COLORADO SPRINGS, COLORADO 80935

The Navigators is an international Christian organization. Jesus Christ gave His followers the Great Commission to go and make disciples (Matthew 28:19). The aim of The Navigators is to help fulfill that commission by multiplying laborers for Christ in every nation.

NavPress is the publishing ministry of The Navigators. NavPress publications are tools to help Christians grow. Although publications alone cannot make disciples or change lives, they can help believers learn biblical discipleship, and apply what they learn to their lives and ministries.

Fifth printing, 1992

Excerpts from *The Blessing* are reprinted by permission of Thomas Nelson Publishers, copyright © 1986, by Gary Smalley and John Trent.

Study guide prepared by Larry K. Weeden.

Unless otherwise noted, all Scripture quotations are from *The New King James Version* (NKJV). Copyright © 1979, 1980, 1982, Thomas Nelson, Inc., Publishers. Another version used is the *Holy Bible: New International Version* (NIV). Copyright © 1973, 1978, 1984, International Bible Society. Used by permission of Zondervan Bible Publishers.

Printed in the United States of America

CONTENTS

AUTHORS

Gary Smalley, president of Today's Family, holds a bachelor's degree in psychology and has a master's degree from Bethel Seminary in St. Paul, Minnesota. His previous books include *If Only He Knew, For Better or for Best, Joy That Lasts,* and *The Key to Your Child's Heart.* He and his wife, Norma, are the parents of three children, Kari, Greg, and Michael.

John Trent, vice president of Today's Family, has a Ph.D. in marriage and family counseling and holds a master's degree from Dallas Theological Seminary. He wrote with Gary the best-selling books *The Language of Love, The Blessing, The Gift of Honor, Love Is a Decision,* and *The Two Sides of Love.* He lives in Phoenix with his wife, Cynthia, and daughters, Kari Lorraine and Laura Catherine.

INTRODUCTION

Each of us has a deep-seated, God-given need to feel blessed. Whether we've ever put it into words or not, we each long to be loved and accepted unconditionally just for who we are, regardless of what we've done or failed to do. If we feel blessed, we can face life with self-confidence and joy. If we lack such a feeling, however—even subconsciously—life is full of frustration, fear, and disappointment.

Ideally, we first get a sense of being blessed early in life from our parents, then later from siblings, friends, teachers, and co-workers. Ultimately, we understand and grow to bask in God's rich blessing, which was demonstrated most clearly in Christ's death for our sins while we were yet sinners in rebellion against Him (see Romans 5:8).

Unfortunately, many of us live far short of that ideal. Often parents, even those with the best intentions, don't know how to convey a sense of blessing to their children. And when we grow up without a sense of parental blessing, it's difficult to feel blessed by anyone else, including God. The book titled *The Blessing* (Thomas Nelson Publishers) has become a best seller precisely because there are so many of us who long to feel blessed, and because many concerned parents want to know how they can be sure their children *will* grow up with a sense of blessing.

The purpose of this guide is to present key principles from that book, then provide questions, self-tests, and other resources to help individuals and small groups think through the issues and their own experiences in light of those principles. Finally, there are exercises designed to help individuals put the lessons learned into practice so they can enjoy emotional and spiritual growth. More specifically, each session of this study guide is divided into the following parts:

"Identifying the Issues." This section presents *The Blessing* in greatly condensed form through an excerpt from the book along with paraphrased stories. The book contains much more helpful information than it was possible to include in this guide. Therefore, reading the book will be important in order for you to fully understand and appreciate what it means to give and receive the blessing.

"Exploring the Issues." In this section are questions and a self-test to help you understand the issues and see how they relate to your own experience. A biblical passage (with questions) that adds to or illustrates the principles covered in the session is also included. Space is provided for writing your answers. If you're using the study in a small group, you and the others will benefit most if you read the excerpt and go through this section on your own before the group study.

"Bringing It Home." This part of the session is meant to help you take the principles discussed in the first two sections and make them a part of your daily life. *Please don't skip this section.* Only by following through with this step will you see the lessons begin to change your life for the better; this is where you put them into action. This section, along with the first two, should easily generate an hour's discussion in a small group setting.

"Taking It Further." In this section are two things designed to promote an even greater depth of understanding of the session's issues and principles. First is a listing of the chapter(s) in *The Blessing* that correspond to the session. Second are thought-provoking quotations related to the topic of the session, with questions after each quotation to help you consider how they illuminate or modify the truths that have been discussed.

This section is entirely optional. It will add to your grasp of

8

the topic, but it isn't essential to a full and adequate understanding and application of the session's principles. It's for those who have extra time and interest in the subject.

This guide can be used for individual study with great benefit. You may gain even more from it, however, if you participate in a small group that works through it together. We can all learn much from the experiences of others, and there's a lot of support to be gained in group fellowship. Experience also shows that in putting lessons learned into practice, we do much better if we feel accountable to others—if we know someone will ask us periodically how we're doing at putting our good intentions into action.

God has seen fit to use *The Blessing* to help many people find emotional healing, the healing of relationships with parents, children, spouses, and friends, and a richer relationship with Himself. It's our prayer that in some unique way, this study guide will help bring the same blessings into your life.

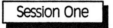

IN SEARCH
OF THE BLESSING

IDENTIFYING THE ISSUES

All of us long to be accepted by others. While we may say out loud, "I don't care what other people think about me," on the inside we all yearn for intimacy and affection. This yearning is especially true in our relationship with our parents. Gaining or missing out on parental approval has a tremendous effect on us, even if it has been years since we have had any regular contact with them. In fact, what happens in our relationship with our parents can greatly affect all our present and future relationships. While this may sound like an exaggeration, our office has been filled with people struggling with this very issue. . . .

. . . [P]eople who are searching for their family's blessing . . . years after they had moved away from home *physically* . . . still [remain] chained to the past *emotionally*. Their lack of approval from their parents in the past [keeps] a feeling of genuine acceptance from others in the present from taking root in their lives. . . .

Some people are driven toward workaholism as they search for the blessing they never received at home. Always striving for acceptance, they never feel satisfied that they are measuring up. Others get mired in withdrawal and apathy as

11

they give up hope of ever truly being blessed. Unfortunately, this withdrawal can become so severe that it can lead to chronic depression and even suicide. For almost all children who miss out on their parents' blessing, at some level this lack of acceptance sets off a lifelong search.

This search for the blessing is not just a modern-day phenomenon. This is actually centuries old. In fact, we can find a graphic picture in the Old Testament of a person who missed out on his family's blessing. This person was a confused and angry man named Esau. . . .

One of the most familiar verses in the Bible is Genesis 2:24: "For this reason a man shall leave his father and his mother, and shall cleave to his wife" (NASB). Many books and tapes talk about the need to cleave to our spouse. However, very few talk about the tremendous need people have to "leave" home. Perhaps this is because people [usually think] of leaving home as simply moving away physically. . . .

The terrible fact is that most people who have missed out on their parents' blessing have great emotional difficulty leaving home. It may have been years since they have seen their parents, but unmet needs for personal acceptance can keep a person emotionally chained to his or her parents' home, unable to genuinely cleave to another person in a lasting relationship. For this reason many couples never get off the ground in terms of marital intimacy. . . . You or a loved one may be facing this problem. Understanding the concept of the blessing is crucial to defeating the problem and freeing people to build healthy relationships.

The stories of Brian and Nancy illustrate people searching for parental blessing. Brian's father had made a career of being a Marine officer, and he raised Brian to follow in his footsteps. To "toughen" Brian, he had never given him approval for any of his athletic or academic achievements. Instead, he always pointed out Brian's mistakes and challenged him to do even better.

When Brian joined the Marines after graduating from high school, his father was overjoyed, but Brian soon got into trouble for attitude problems and fighting. Eventually, he was dishonorably discharged from the Corps. As soon as that happened, he was no longer welcome at home, and communication with his father stopped.

In the years that followed, Brian struggled with feelings of inferiority and found it impossible to form lasting relationships. He didn't believe another person could love him. His father died before there was any reconciliation between them, leaving Brian heartbroken.

Nancy was a tomboy, but her mother wanted a petite little lady. Nancy's younger sister, who was more to her mother's liking, became the favorite. Nancy was often belittled by her mother for being overweight and was compared unfavorably to her sister. Eventually Nancy was left at home when her mother and her sister went out to various social events.

When Nancy grew up, she struggled constantly with her weight and low self-esteem. But she married and had two daughters of her own. Like Nancy and her sister, the older girl was bigger and looked a lot like Nancy, while the younger was beautiful and petite. And as it had been in Nancy's childhood, Nancy's mother favored the younger, petite granddaughter, often ignoring the older girl. It was painful for Nancy to realize that she was becoming resentful and bitter toward her younger daughter.

EXPLORING THE ISSUES

1. How would you define this concept of a family "blessing"?

2. What are some of the common consequences of lacking this blessing, according to the excerpt and/or your observations?

3. Can you remember a time in your life when you clearly felt you had the blessing of one or both of your parents? What did they say or do to give you that feeling?

4. The following self-test will help you determine whether you live with or without a sense of your parents' blessing. It consists of seven yes/no questions for you to answer. A yes answer to one question may indicate that you feel you lack their blessing; a yes answer to two or more questions is a strong indication you feel that way.

a. Are your parents frequently critical of you or your lifestyle? ___ yes ___ no

b. In most decisions you make, do you consider what your parents will think? ___ yes ___ no

c. Would you or others say you're a workaholic? ___ yes ___ no

d. Do you feel your mom or dad prefers a brother or sister over you? ___ yes ___ no

e. When you are with your parents, are you usually on edge, waiting for some conflict to erupt? ___ yes ___ no

f. Are you pursuing any major goals because you know they will please your parents? ___ yes ___ no

g. Do you sometimes feel that no matter how hard you work or how much you achieve, you will never be satisfied? ___ yes ___ no

5. How is a person who feels a lack of parental blessing likely to feel about God? Why?

6. Genesis 27:1-40 shows how Esau lost his father's blessing and how that affected him. Read that passage and then answer the following questions.

a. How did Jacob steal the blessing meant for Esau?

b. How did Esau respond?

c. What was Isaac's response?

d. How did the two blessings given to Jacob and Esau differ?

e. Who are some other biblical people who seemed to suffer from a lack of parental blessing?

7. What problems might exist in a marriage in which one or both spouses have failed to "leave home" emotionally?

8. To what extent are Brian and Nancy the products of their environments, and to what extent are they responsible for their own dilemmas?

9. Describe the attitudes and behavior of a person who has and feels the blessing of his parents.

10. Describe a marriage in which both partners feel blessed.

BRINGING IT HOME

The principles presented in this session need to be made personal if you want to see the greatest positive impact in your life. The questions and suggestions in this section are designed to help you transform truth into action.

1. If at this point you think you did not receive your parents' blessing, pray now and ask God to forgive them. Ask Him to also help *you* to forgive them if there's a root of bitterness in your heart.

2. Who in your life should you be blessing today? Make a list. Your list might include your spouse, your children, your parents, co-workers, people at church, neighbors, and so on. As we look in detail in future sessions at what the blessing involves, begin to pray now that God will show you how to be a real blessing to those people. Make that request a daily prayer throughout this study.

3. In preparation for the next session, list some practical things a person could say or do that would convey a sense of blessing to others. Then compare your list to the elements of the blessing as explained in the next session and be ready to add your insights to the discussion.

TAKING IT FURTHER

The following resources are entirely optional, meant for those who want to go beyond the session and take its ideas even further. Choose those that interest you; feel free to pass over the rest.

1. Read chapter 1 of *The Blessing.*

2. Read the following quotations, and answer the questions after each.

a. "Children have never been good at listening to their parents, but they have never failed to imitate them." (James Baldwin)

▶What are the best traits of your parents that you see in yourself? What are the worst?

▶If you have children, which of your traits do you see most clearly in them?

b. "When adults realize that every human being— especially the adolescent—hungers for understanding, acceptance, and recognition, many of the problems of delinquency will be on their way to solution." (William A. Ward)

▶Do you agree or disagree with that statement? Why?

▶What would be the likely consequences for society if more people felt blessed by their parents?

c. "Society creates the myth that marriage is the proper haven for all our longings and a cure for all our shortcomings. People are programmed to believe that marriage will automatically give them individuality, identity, security, and happiness, when as a matter of fact marriage gives them none of these things unless they possess them in the first place." (Gerald Griffin)

▶What can we realistically expect of marriage in terms of meeting our emotional needs?

▶To what extent do unrealistic expectations cause marital discord?

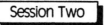

THE BLESSING:
YESTERDAY AND TODAY

IDENTIFYING THE ISSUES

. . . Every flower needs soil, air, water, light, and a secure place to grow (one where its roots are not constantly being pulled out). When these five basic ingredients are present, it is almost impossible to keep a flower from growing. The same thing is true when it comes to the basic elements of the blessing.

Like the basic needs a flower has, the blessing also has five key elements. These five elements, blended together, can cause personal acceptance to blossom and grow in our home today. Each individual part provides a unique contribution. Each is needed in giving the blessing. . . .

A definition of the blessing that contains its five major elements reads: A family blessing begins with *meaningful touching*. It continues with a *spoken message* of high value, a message that pictures a *special future* for the individual being blessed, and one that is based on an *active commitment* to see the blessing come to pass. . . .

Meaningful touch was an essential element in bestowing the blessing in Old Testament homes. So it was with Isaac when he went to bless his son. We read in Genesis 27:26 that Isaac said, "Come near now and kiss me, my son." This

19

incident was not an isolated one. Each time the blessing was given in the Scriptures, meaningful touching provided a caring background to the words that would be spoken. Kissing, hugging, or the laying on of hands were all a part of bestowing the blessing. . . .

The second element of our definition is based on a spoken message. In many homes today, words of love and acceptance are seldom heard. A tragic misconception parents in these homes share is that simply being present communicates the blessing. Nothing could be further from the truth. A blessing becomes so only when it is spoken. . . .

[The third element is attaching high value.] To value something means to attach honor to it. In fact, this is the meaning of the verb "to bless." In Hebrew, the word *bless* literally means "to bow the knee." This word was used in showing reverence, even awe, to an important person. Now, this doesn't mean that in order to bless a person we are to stand back, fall to our knees, and bow before that person in awe! Nonetheless, words of blessing should carry with them the recognition that this person is valuable and has redeeming qualities. . . .

A fourth element of the blessing is the way it pictures a special future for the person being blessed. Isaac says to his son Jacob, "May God give you/ Of the dew of heaven,/ Of the fatness of the earth. . . . Let peoples serve you,/ And nations bow down to you" (Gen. 27:28-29). Even today, Jewish homes are noted for picturing a special future for their children. . . .

The last element of the blessing pictures the *responsibility* that goes with giving the blessing. For the patriarchs, not only their words, but God Himself stood behind the blessing they bestowed on their children. . . .

Parents today, in particular, need to rely on the Lord to give them the strength and staying power to confirm their children's blessing. . . .

The blessing of children that began with the patriarchs continued through the centuries of Jewish life. In Mark 10:13-16 we also see Jesus blessing children. Even today, in many orthodox synagogues, a special blessing for children is often a part of *Shabat* (Sabbath) services.

1. Which one of these five elements of the blessing was most present in your childhood home? Which one was least present?

2. The following exercise will help you measure how evident each element is in your home today. If you're single, think in terms of your relationship with your parents. By circling the appropriate number on a scale from 1 (very little) to 5 (a lot), indicate how much you see of each element.

Meaningful touch	1	2	3	4	5
Spoken message	1	2	3	4	5
Attaching high value	1	2	3	4	5
Picturing a special future	1	2	3	4	5
Active commitment	1	2	3	4	5

3. Which element would you most like to see *more of* in your own home? Why?

4. Is it possible for people to have a sense of being blessed even if one or more of these elements is missing? Why or why not?

5. In Genesis 48:8-20, Jacob blessed two of his grandsons, the children of Joseph, shortly before Jacob died. Read that portion of Scripture and answer these questions:

a. Does this passage picture all five elements of the blessing? Where? Which, if any, seem to be missing?

b. In blessing the two boys, what did Jacob do that was unusual? Why did he do it?

c. Imagine yourself as Ephraim receiving such a blessing from a godly, elderly grandfather. What feelings would it create in you?

6. Does the need to provide meaningful, loving touch mean that spanking is bad? Why or why not? (You might want to refer to Proverbs 13:24, 23:13-14, and 29:15.)

7. Besides "I love you," what are some things we can say to people that convey the blessing?

8. What innate qualities or characteristics give all people value regardless of who they are or what they've done?

9. What picture of your future did your parents give you?

10. In what ways does God demonstrate His active commitment to us?

BRINGING IT HOME
---

1. Review your answer to question 3. Pray that God would increase that element in your family life.

2. Think of one new way to put that element into action during the coming week. Pray that God would strengthen you with love and courage to do more of it every day.

3. In preparation for the next session, list some people who would probably appreciate an occasional friendly touch from you—a warm handshake, a pat on the shoulder, a hug.

1. Read chapter 2 in *The Blessing.*
2. Read the following quotations, and answer the accompanying questions:

> a. "Parents are prone to give their children everything except the one thing they need most. That is time: time for listening, time for understanding, time for helping, and time for guiding. It sounds simple, but in reality it is the most difficult, and the most sacrificial task of parenthood." (Emma K. Hulburt)
>
> ▶What are the highest priorities in your life?
> ▶How much time do you spend on them in a typical week?
> ▶Which of your time commitments accurately reflect your values, and which do not?
>
> b. "Take from a man his wealth, and you hinder him; take from him his purpose, and you slow him down. But take from a man his hope, and you stop him. He can go on without wealth, and even without purpose, for a while. But he will not go on without hope." (C. Neil Strait)
>
> ▶Think of a person you know who seems to have no particular hope for the future. What's his outlook on life?
> ▶Compare that to the outlook of someone whose parents pictured a positive future for him or her.
>
> c. "Everybody needs a hug. It changes your metabolism." (Leo Buscaglia)
>
> ▶How do you feel when you receive a friendly touch from someone you care about?
> ▶If you have a family or close friends, how do you think they feel when you give them a meaningful touch?
> ▶Do you feel comfortable with touching and being touched? Why or why not?

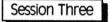

THE FIRST ELEMENT OF THE BLESSING: MEANINGFUL TOUCH

IDENTIFYING THE ISSUES

. . . Even in caring homes, most parents (particularly fathers) will stop touching their children once the children reach the grade school years. When they do stop touching them, an important part of giving their children the blessing stops as well.

For a four-year-old, being held and touched is permissible in most homes. But what about the need a fourteen-year-old has to be meaningfully touched by his mother or father? (Even if the teenager outwardly cringes every time he or she is hugged.) Or a thirty-four-year-old? Or your spouse or a close friend?

Your spouse and others need meaningful touch. However, children are particularly affected by touch deprivation. Sometimes the absence of touch can so affect a child that he or she spends a lifetime reaching out for arms that will never embrace him or her. . . .

. . . There are at least two important reasons why placing our hands on someone as a part of the blessing is so special. First, there is a symbolic meaning attached to touching, and, second, there are tremendous physical benefits to the laying on of hands. . . .

. . . Studies show that touching can actually lower a person's blood pressure. Low blood pressure is an important part of staying healthy. But that's not all. In a recent study at UCLA, it was found that just to maintain emotional and physical health, men and women need eight to ten meaningful touches each day! . . .

This study estimated that if some "type A driven" men would hug their wives several times each day, it would increase their life span by almost two years! (Not to mention the way it would improve their marriages.) . . .

Touching a child on the shoulder when he or she walks in front of you; holding hands with your spouse when you wait in line; stopping for a moment to ruffle someone's hair—all these small acts can change how you are viewed by others. A ten-minute bear hug is not the only way to give another person the blessing. At times, the smallest act of touch can be a vehicle to communicating love and personal acceptance. . . .

Parents, in particular, need to know that neglecting to meaningfully touch their children starves them of genuine acceptance—so much so that it can drive them into the arms of someone else who is all too willing to touch them. . . .

Promiscuous men and women, women who work as prostitutes, and women who repeatedly have unwanted pregnancies have told researchers that their sexual activity is merely a way of satisfying yearnings to be touched and held.

Other studies have shown that meaningful touch is healthy for newborn infants as well as elderly people in nursing homes. Touching increases the hemoglobin level in the blood of both the toucher and the one being touched, invigorating body tissues with more oxygen. Thus, meaningful touch has a very positive, important effect both physically and emotionally.

EXPLORING THE ISSUES

1. Define the phrase *meaningful touch*.

2. What are some positive messages that can be conveyed by touch?

3. Describe a time when a parent or grandparent held or touched you in such a way, perhaps without even saying a word, that you felt especially loved.

4.   a. Are you conscious of a need in your life for more meaningful touches? How do you know?

   b. Are you aware of anyone else who has such a need, maybe in your own family? How do you recognize it?

5. Mark 10:13-16 shows Jesus interacting with some people, including children. Read that passage and answer the following:

   a. What elements of the blessing do we see in Jesus' response to the children?

b. What does this scene say about Jesus' personality? (Have you ever known kids to be attracted to a grump?)

c. What are some other examples of loving touch in the Bible? (See Isaiah 6:5-7, Mark 5:25-34, Mark 5:35-42, Acts 3:1-7, Romans 16:16, and 1 Thessalonians 5:26.)

d. Eighty percent of a woman's physical needs are non-sexual. Yet that area of married life is important. Read Song of Solomon 5:16 and 6:1-3 and Hebrews 13:4.

6. Read the following five statements and check whether you agree or disagree. In a discussion group, explain why you chose your particular answer.

a. The need for loving touch is as real and legitimate as our need for food, water, and sleep. __ agree __ disagree

b. The culture in which one lives has a major bearing on what kinds of touch are acceptable or appropriate.
__ agree __ disagree

c. Touching people of the opposite sex, with the exception of close family members, always has sexual overtones. __ agree __ disagree

d. What is acceptable as friendly touch has changed significantly in the past thirty years. __ agree __ disagree

e. If a person has not received meaningful touches at home, we should judge sympathetically if he or she seeks those touches elsewhere. __ agree __ disagree

28

7. a. Is it appropriate for a church in some way to try to meet people's need for meaningful touch? Why or why not?

b. How might it try?

8. What are some commonsense guidelines that should govern our use of meaningful touch?

9. Although we don't feel a physical touch from God, in what ways can we be aware of His reaching out to us in love in our daily lives? (Read two of the following psalms: 32, 34, 103, 139.)

BRINGING IT HOME
---

1. During one normal day next week, count how many meaningful touches you receive and how many you give. If either number is less than you'd like, make an effort to increase the number *you give out* in the next week.

2. Think of one person outside your closest circle of friends who you realize does not receive much loving touch. Pray about how you could reach out to that person, both figuratively and literally, and plan to begin reaching out in some way in the next two weeks.

3. In preparation for the next session, take special note one day of your conversations with family members or others close to you. Analyze them along these lines: How much time did I spend talking to each person? Who did most of the talking? Was the basic nature of the conversation with each person positive, negative, or neutral?

TAKING IT FURTHER

1. Read chapter 3 in *The Blessing*.
2. Read the statements that follow, and answer the related questions.

a. "If you observe those who have deep relationships, you will find that, although few of them are indiscriminate grabbers who hug everyone in sight, most have delicately tuned their sense of touch, and it is in use every time they are with people. They listen with their eyes, they draw close to another person during conversation, and they make body contact frequently to keep the communication at a warm level." (Alan Loy McGinnis)
▶Who do you know that relates to people like this?
▶How do you feel when he or she is talking to you? Why?

b. "Surprisingly, studies show that most parents touch their children only when necessity demands it. . . . Otherwise few parents take advantage of this pleasant, effortless way of giving their children that unconditional love they so desperately need. . . . These parents don't know the fantastic opportunities they are missing. Within their hands they have a way of assuring their children's emotional security and their own success as parents." (Ross Campbell)
▶If you're a parent, how often do you hug your child, stroke his or her hair, or pat him or her on the back? Is

it as often as you'd like?

▶For what reasons do you hold back from doing it more?

c. "A man with leprosy came to [Jesus] and begged him on his knees, 'If you are willing, you can make me clean.' Filled with compassion, Jesus reached out his hand and touched the man. 'I am willing,' he said. 'Be clean!' Immediately the leprosy left him and he was cured." (Mark 1:40-42, NIV)

▶Since Jesus could have healed the man *without* touching him, why do you think He chose to touch him?

▶What, if anything, does this say to us about how we should relate to people who are sick or outcast?

THE SECOND ELEMENT OF THE BLESSING: SPOKEN WORDS

IDENTIFYING THE ISSUES

Words have incredible power to build us up or tear us down emotionally. This is particularly true when it comes to giving or gaining family approval. Many people can clearly remember words of praise their parents spoke years ago. Others can remember negative words they heard—and what their parents were wearing when they spoke them!

We should not be surprised, then, that the family blessing hinges on being a *spoken* message. Abraham *spoke* a blessing to Isaac. Isaac *spoke* it to his son Jacob. Jacob *spoke* it to each of his twelve sons and to two of his grandchildren. Esau was so excited when he was called in to receive his blessing because, after years of waiting, he would finally hear the blessing. In the Scriptures, a blessing is not a blessing unless it is spoken. . . .

If you are a parent, your children desperately need to *hear* a spoken blessing from you. If you are married, your wife or husband needs to hear words of love and accept-ance on a regular basis. This very week . . . you will rub shoulders with someone who needs to hear a word of encouragement. . . .

A thief is loose in many homes today who masquerades

as "fulfillment," "accomplishment," and "success." Actually, this thief steals from our children the precious gift of genuine acceptance and leaves confusion and emptiness in its place. That villain's name is *overactivity*, and it can keep parents so busy that the blessing is never spoken. Even with parents who dearly love their children, as one woman we talked to said, "Who has time to stop and *tell* them?"

In many homes today, both parents are working overtime, and a "family night" makes an appearance about as often as Halley's comet. The result is that instead of Dad and Mom taking the time to communicate a spoken blessing, a babysitter named *silence* is left to mold a child's self-perception. . . .

Both praise and criticism seem to trickle down through generations. If you never heard words of love and acceptance, expect to struggle with speaking them yourself. . . .

Spoken words—many times we have to be facing the pressure of time before we say the things closest to our hearts. . . . [W]ith your children, your spouse, your close friends, even with your parents, it's later than you think. In some relationships, it is already late afternoon in your opportunity to talk to them.

When parents fail to speak words of blessing, their children are often driven in one of two directions. They may become workaholics, striving endlessly to earn parental praise. Or they may withdraw, totally giving up in their attempts to earn Mom and Dad's approval.

When negative words are spoken to someone, even jokingly, they can mark that person for life. "Mean Mike" was named by his parents when he was just a toddler; when anyone would try to take something from him, he would snarl and hang on tight. Originally, the nickname was just their funny way of describing this trait. But as Mike grew older, the name stuck, and tragically he tried to live up to his reputation.

Mike became a bully in school and a "tough guy" in his relationships. Little by little, his character grew to match his nickname. Today Mike is in a state prison in Arizona. Many experiences contributed to his being there, one of which was a nickname spoken in jest.

1.   a. When you were growing up, what was the practice in your family about communicating love and blessing to one another?

b. What effect did this have on your perception of your parents' feelings for you?

c. How did it affect your ability to speak words of blessing to others?

2.   a. What is common regarding words of love and encouragement in your own home today? Why?

b. Is that what you want?

3. Do you find it easy or hard to *accept* words of blessing? Why?

4. The Apostle James talked about the effect of words in chapter 3, verses 3-6, of his epistle. Read that passage, then answer the following questions.

   a. What does this passage say about the power of the tongue?

   b. In what ways can words steer a life?

   c. Is the power of the tongue used most often for good or for evil? Why?

5.   **a.** Describe a time when you surprised someone—or someone surprised you—with words of love or encouragement. How did the person—or you—react?

   b. Read the book of Philemon. How do you think Onesimus felt?

6. Is there anyone in your life with whom it seems to be "late afternoon" in your opportunity to speak words of blessing? What are the obstacles you face in doing so?

7. List some words of acceptance and encouragement that you can offer to those you see daily.

8. What are some specific words of blessing—just one statement of love, encouragement, or acceptance—that you can share with the people closest to you? Write them out here.

Spouse

Child

Parent

Sibling

Friend

Co-worker

Neighbor

Pastor or spiritual teacher

Other (your choice)

9. When a family night or other planned time for spoken blessings isn't practical, how can busy parents meet this need

▶for their children?

▶for each other?

<hr>
BRINGING IT HOME

1. Sometime this week, find an opportunity to share with each person your blessing listed in question 8 on pages 37-38.

2. Pray that God would give you greater sensitivity to others who need your blessing. Pray especially about how you can offer healing words of encouragement to someone who's hurting right now or with whom you've had a difficult relationship.

3. In preparation for the next session, think of the people closest to you and what you most appreciate, or value, about each of them. Have you conveyed that appreciation in words?

<hr>
TAKING IT FURTHER

1. Read chapter 4 in *The Blessing.*
2. Read the following statements, and then answer the questions.

a. "'Everyone who calls on the name of the Lord will be saved.' How, then, can they call on the one they have not believed in? And how can they believe in the one of whom they have not heard? And how can they hear without someone preaching to them?" (Romans 10:13-14, NIV)

▶Might the idea of a spoken blessing include telling people about Jesus? Why or why not?

▶Who is there in your closest circle of family and friends with whom you've never had a serious conversation about the claims of Christ?

b. "Man does not live by words alone, despite the fact that sometimes he has to eat them." (Adlai Stevenson)

▶Think of a time when you said something you instantly regretted. Were you able to repair the damage done?

▶If so, how, and how long did it take?

c. "The 10 most persuasive words in the English language are: you, easy, money, save, love, new, discovery, results, proven, guarantee." (Henry J. Tayor)

▶What makes these words so persuasive?

▶What are some other powerful words? (Refer to James 3:1-12 to stimulate your thinking.)

THE THIRD ELEMENT OF THE BLESSING: EXPRESSING HIGH VALUE

IDENTIFYING THE ISSUES

. . . [T]o "value" something means to attach great importance to it. This is at the very heart of the concept of "blessing." In Hebrew, to "bow the knee" is the root meaning of blessing. . . . In relationship to God, the word came to mean "to adore with bended knees." Bowing before someone is a graphic picture of valuing that person. . . .

. . . When words of value are linked only to a child's performance, they lose much of their impact. Children who have to perform to get a blessing retain a nagging uncertainty about whether they ever really received it. If their performance ever drops even a small amount, they can ask and re-ask, "Am I loved for 'who I am' or only for 'what I can do'?"

We need to find a better way to communicate a message of high value and acceptance. . . . Hidden inside the family blessing is a key to communicating such feelings . . . a key we can perfect with only a little practice. . . . This key is found in the way word pictures are used throughout the Scriptures. . . .

. . . "Behold, you are fair, my love!/Behold, you are fair!/You have dove's eyes behind your veil" (Song of Sol. 4:1). . . .

41

What Solomon does with his word picture (and what a wise parent does in blessing his or her child) is to try to capture a character trait or physical attribute of his beloved in an everyday object. In this case, he pictures her eyes as [a] dove's. The gentle, shy, and tender nature of these creatures would be familiar to his bride. . . . Plus, an added feature is that each time she saw a dove thereafter, it would remind her of how her husband viewed her and valued her. . . .

The second key: . . . Over and over Solomon uses everyday objects that capture the emotional meaning behind the trait he wants to praise. . . .

Solomon gained a third thing by using . . . the ability word pictures have to get around the defenses of insecure or defensive people and to get across a message of high value. . . .

Jesus knew the importance of using word pictures with those who were timid of heart. He would talk about being the Good Shepherd who watched over the flock; the true vine that could bring spiritual sustenance; and the bread of life that would provide spiritual nourishment. By using everyday objects, He was able to penetrate the walls of insecurity and mistrust these people had put up, because stories hold a key to our hearts that simple words do not. . . .

A fourth reason for using word pictures is to illustrate the undeveloped traits of a person. Jesus did this in changing Simon's name to Peter (literally "rock" in Greek). . . .

Jenny knows the power of word pictures to express value and blessing. She was divorced by her adulterous husband and left with two small children and no job skills. She struggled to meet life's increased demands, but today she has a good job that meets her family's needs and allows her time to spend with her children.

When asked what was her greatest source of help during the first difficult years after the divorce, she replied, "The Lord was certainly the greatest source of help to us when Jack first left; but from a human perspective, I would have to point to my father. Every time I wanted to quit school or just give up, he would say to me, 'You'll make it, Jenny. You're my rock of Gibraltar. I know you'll make it.' I didn't feel like a rock at the time. My whole world seemed to be caving in. But it helped me so much to know that he pictured me this way. It gave me the hope that maybe I could make it."[1]

EXPLORING THE ISSUES
---

1.   a. What gives you the greatest sense of value? (Is it what people say about you or what you accomplish?)

b. Write a word picture that conveys the way you feel when valued.

2. The following is a true/false self-test designed to help firm up in your understanding some of the ideas related to word pictures.[2] Read each statement and then check true or false. If you're not sure of an answer, go back and review the opening excerpt.

a. A word picture should capture a good trait, and also the positive emotion behind the trait.   __ true __ false

b. To avoid inflating others' egos, words of value should only be given when they're earned by performance.
__ true __ false

c. Jesus and Solomon used word pictures because the people of their day were simple in their understanding.
__ true __ false

d. Word pictures are a way of getting through the defenses of insecure or even hostile people.
__ true __ false

e. To make them more memorable, word pictures should employ unusual or unfamiliar objects and images.

___ true ___ false

f. Word pictures can express appreciation not only for what a person is, but also for what he or she might become. ___ true ___ false

g. Word pictures don't work well with people who aren't creative in their thinking. ___ true ___ false

3. In Genesis 49:9-10,21-22, we see portions of three of the blessings bestowed by Jacob on his sons. Read those verses and then answer these questions:

a. What qualities or symbols in the word picture given to Judah would offer him a sense of high value?

b. What element of prophecy is there in the blessing of Judah?

c. What positive self-images would Naphtali and Joseph have received from their blessings?

4. What are some everyday objects that might be used to picture such positive traits as loyalty, compassion, and energy?

5. In a previous session, we saw how the nickname "Mean Mike" brought out the worst in that young man's potential; what are some names of endearment that might point out a person's positive potential?

6. Since there's a danger in expressing words of value only when people perform well, what are some other times when we might want to convey such a message?

7. What are some creative ways—besides face-to-face conversation—of expressing high value to others?

8.   a. Might it ever be appropriate to use negative word pictures as a way of pointing out a bad trait or character flaw? Why or why not?[3]

    b. If the answer is yes, what guidelines should be followed to make them beneficial rather than harmful?

9. What can we do when we don't *feel* like expressing high value to someone, even though we know we should?

BRINGING IT HOME
---

1. Think of a timid or insecure person you know who might be helped by words of high value. What kind of word picture might work with this particular person?

2. In the next week, pick out a positive trait or potential in each of the people closest to you, and ask God to help you express high value to them regularly for those things.

3. In preparation for the next session, spend a few minutes analyzing whether your basic outlook on the future is positive or negative. Why do you think it's the way it is? A self-test in the next lesson will assist your analysis.

TAKING IT FURTHER
---

1. Read chapter 5 in *The Blessing*.
2. Read these quotations, then answer the questions that follow.

    a. "It is easy to complain and criticize because you are upset and your anger motivates you, but to stand up and call a good job a 'good job' . . . is a truly rewarding pastime. You cannot possibly make another person as happy as you make yourself." (Arthur Fettig)
    ▶How do you feel when someone compliments you?
    ▶How do others usually react when you compliment them? How does *that* make you feel?

b. "A person may not be as good as you tell him he is, but he'll try harder thereafter." (Unknown)

▶What is it about compliments or recognition that makes us try harder?

▶Which has the longer-lasting effect, a criticism or a compliment? Why?

c. "[Jesus'] use of parables was a calculated effort on His part to get His listeners to think about what He was saying rather than spend their time enjoying the way He said it." (D. Stuart Briscoe)

▶In what ways were Jesus' parables like word pictures?

▶In what ways were they different from word pictures?

▶Why did some people learn from His parables and many others did not? (See Matthew 13:13-17 and John 2:18-25.)

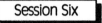

THE FOURTH ELEMENT OF THE BLESSING: PICTURING A SPECIAL FUTURE

IDENTIFYING THE ISSUES

When it comes to predictions about their future, children are literalists—particularly when they hear predictions from their parents, the most important people from an earthly perspective, in their lives. For this reason, communicating a special future to a child is such an important part of giving the blessing. When a person feels in his or her heart that the future is hopeful and something to look forward to, it can greatly affect his or her attitude [about] life. . . .

Children begin to take steps down the positive pathway pictured for them when they hear words like these: "God has given you such a sensitive heart. I wouldn't be surprised if you end up helping a great many people when you grow older," or "You are such a good helper. When you grow up and marry someday, you're going to be such a help to your wife (or husband) and family." On the other hand, just the opposite is true as well. . . .

Words that picture a special future for a child . . . stimulate all kinds of positive feelings and decisions within a child that can help him or her grow and develop. With words of a special future, a child can begin to work on a particular talent, have the confidence to try out for a school

49

office, or even share his or her faith with other children. But . . . [e]motional, physical, and even spiritual growth . . . can be stunted because of the stifling effect of a negative picture of the future. . . .

Because God has been reliable in the past, His words of a special future for us in the present have credence. The same principle is true in our desire to provide a special future for those we wish to bless. Our credibility in the past will directly affect how our words are received in the present. . . .

Perhaps your past has been anything but consistent with those you want to bless. Today really is the first day of the rest of your life. And you can begin to build the kind of "past" that words of a special future need to rest on by honoring commitments to your children today. . . .

Words of a special future for a child can dissolve into ashes when a husband or wife walks out on a relationship. . . . For those of you who are married, an important part of picturing a special future for your children is keeping your present commitment to your spouse strong and intact.

Ted was a good example of someone whose credibility suffered because his actions were inconsistent with his words. A sales manager for a national company, he was away on business more than he was home. And although he did a good job of picturing a special future for his two children *with words*, his demanding schedule, coupled with fatigue when he was home, kept him from following through on his promises.

For example, he had noticed that his daughter had a great love of animals. So he would say to her, "Samantha, we're going to get a horse for you so you can ride it and take care of it. You might even become a veterinarian someday!" Soon, however, Ted was on the road again and never followed through.

After nine years, Ted realized he would have to cut back on his traveling if he were going to have a secure marriage and family. To do this, he took a different job and accepted a cut in pay. But by now his children no longer listened to his promises, and their lives, for the most part, excluded him. As far as they were concerned, he had nothing to do with the future.

Fortunately, Ted understood the need to build a record of honored commitments with his kids, and patiently did so. It took almost two years, but he finally earned their trust as a man of his word. They realized that he really was interested in them and their potential. Even Samantha's interest in animals was rekindled!

Marcia was blessed by her parents and the special future they pictured for her. She was labeled a "slow learner," and every year of school was a struggle for her. Her parents noticed, however, that she had a gift for encouraging her younger sisters and neighborhood children and explaining things to them in a way they could understand. So they challenged her to develop that gift by letting her help them teach young children in Sunday school.

After working with the children at church one Sunday, Marcia told her parents that she wanted to be a teacher when she grew up. They could have responded by warning her to be "more realistic"; after all, report cards had just been sent home, and Marcia was still at the bottom of her class. Instead, they told her that if she worked hard and kept trying, she *could* be a teacher.

The usual four years of college took Marcia six and a half years to complete, but finally she earned her degree in elementary education. And while many of her college classmates were beginning to look for jobs, Marcia already had one! She did such an outstanding job of student teaching that the principal of the school asked her to come back full-time when she graduated. Her determination, coupled with the encouragement of her parents, made her dream for the future come true.

EXPLORING THE ISSUES

---

1. a. In what way was the future your parents pictured for you positive or negative, hopeful or hopeless?

b. Why do you think they gave you that kind of picture?

2. To gauge your present perspective on the future, rate your feelings about the following statements on a scale from 1 (disagree strongly) to 5 (agree strongly):

a. When I encounter a new problem, I'm confident I'll be able to find a solution.   1   2   3   4   5

b. My key relationships will be stronger a year from now.
                                                      1   2   3   4   5

c. With all the trouble and uncertainty in the world, this isn't a good time to start a family.   1   2   3   4   5

d. I'll be better off financially in two years than I am now.
                                                      1   2   3   4   5

e. If I were to lose my job, my first response would be panic.   1   2   3   4   5

f. The hope of Heaven seems pale compared to my current troubles.   1   2   3   4   5

g. In spite of all the pressures, I believe I can be a successful parent.   1   2   3   4   5

h. I'm sure I can still make my dreams come true.
                                                      1   2   3   4   5

If you generally agree (numbers 3-5) with statements a, b, d, g, and h, your outlook on the future is positive, especially if your choices for statements c, e, and f are low (1-2). On the other hand, if you generally agree with statements c, e, and f, your outlook is negative, especially if your choices are low on statements a, b, d, g, and h.

3. In Jeremiah 29:11 and John 14:2-3, we get a broad view of how God wants us to feel about the future. Read those passages, and then answer these questions:

a. How does God want us to view the future?

b. Do these verses mean we should expect trouble-free lives? Why or why not? (Read Hebrews 11 to gain insight.)

c. Do you have trouble believing God's promises of a bright future? Why or why not?

4. If you have children, what kind of future are you picturing for them now? Why?

5. If you're married and a parent, do your children have reason to believe in or to doubt your commitment to your spouse? Why?

6. How does picturing a special future apply

▶to your spouse?

▶to your parents?

▶to your friends?

7. Has your experience with those closest to you given you credibility in trying to picture a special future for them now? If not, what can you do to begin building credibility?

8. Besides saying words that picture a special future, what practical ways are there for a parent to help a child develop traits or abilities that can lead to a happy future?

9. a. If a parent sees a child, or someone sees a friend, pursuing interests that seem inconsistent with his or her traits or talents, should the parent or friend try to redirect the person's interests? Why or why not?

b. How might they try to do that?

c. How far should they go in trying?

10. If you have a negative view of the future, what ideas or actions might help turn it around?

11. a. List four to six very important people in your life and one way you can picture a special future for each person.

b. How can you help that future become reality for each person?

BRINGING IT HOME

1. If you personally feel uncertain or even negative about the future, make that a subject of daily prayer. Also read a few biblical promises each day for the next month. (You might begin with the following list of references. Also, your pastor or local Christian bookseller can direct you to books based on these promises; for example, Charles Spurgeon's devotional book *Faith's Checkbook*.)

Psalm 2	Matthew 6:25-34	2 Corinthians 4:7-18
Psalm 23	Matthew 7:7-11	Ephesians 1:1-12
Psalm 34	John 3:16	Philippians 1:6
Psalm 37	John 10:27-29	1 Thessalonians 4:14-18
Psalm 91	John 14:1-4	2 Timothy 4:7-8
Psalm 110	John 17	Hebrews 11
Proverbs 3:5-6	Romans 8:18	James 1:2-4
Isaiah 40	Romans 8:28	
Matthew 5:1-12	Romans 8:35-39	

2. Who is the person nearest you who seems to be suffering most from a negative outlook on his or her own future? Plan how you can begin in the next week to bless that person with a new, positive outlook, perhaps by using word pictures.

56

3. In preparation for the next session, try to think of someone—perhaps in your primary or adolescent years—who encouraged you and went out of his or her way to help you over a period of months or even years.

▶What has been this person's lasting impact on your life?

▶If he or she is still living, how can you communicate your gratitude to that person?

TAKING IT FURTHER

1. Read chapter 6 in *The Blessing.*

2. Read the following quotations, and answer the questions after each.

a. "To travel hopefully is better than to arrive." (Sir James Jeans)

▶Do you tend to view each day as a step in a path or as a "destination" in and of itself? Why?

▶How do you feel when you finally reach a goal for which you've worked long and hard? Why?

b. "Parents are not obligated to give their children a secure future, but they are obligated to give them a secure foundation on which to build their own futures." (Unknown)

▶What is the parents' role in preparing a child for the future?

▶Can children build a secure future if they start with an insecure foundation? Why or why not?

c. "Never be afraid to trust an unknown future to a known God." (Corrie ten Boom)

▶How do we find the balance between the need to plan well and the need to step out in faith? (Read Genesis 12, Proverbs 16:9, Hebrews 11:8-19, and James 4:13-16.)

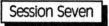

Session Seven

THE FIFTH ELEMENT OF THE BLESSING: ACTIVE COMMITMENT

What do we mean by "active commitment," and why is it such an important part of the blessing? Commitment is important because as we have seen . . . words of blessing alone are not enough. They need to be backed by the commitment of a person to see the blessing come to pass. . . .

The first step: Commit the person being blessed to the Lord. . . .

[An] important reason to commit our children to the Lord when we bless them is that this teaches them that God is personally concerned with their life and welfare. Stressing the fact that the Lord is interested in their being blessed is like introducing them to someone who can be their best friend, a personal encourager they can draw close to throughout their lives. . . .

The second step: Commit our lives to their best interests. . . .

In our homes, we can be people who are close in terms of proximity to each other, but far away in terms of understanding the other person's real desires, needs, goals, hopes, and fears. However, we can combat this by taking the time to understand the unique aspects of those we wish to bless.

Blessing our children involves understanding their unique bent. . . .

. . . While it may seem the very opposite of "blessing" another person, in actuality we bless our children by providing them with appropriate discipline. . . .

. . . If we genuinely love someone, we will not allow him or her to stray into sin or be hurt in some way without trying to correct our loved one. . . .

Third step: Become a student of those we wish to bless. . . .

We would like to give you some practical help in how you can become a student of your children, spouse, or others. One thing that can greatly help is to be lovingly persistent in communicating with them. . . .

. . . [A] second step toward becoming a student of those we wish to bless [is] the importance of shared activities. Not only do they draw us closer together, but sharing activities with our children offers tremendous opportunities to learn about [them]. . . .

Finally, we should talk with friends of those we want to bless. By doing so, we will gain additional insight into their likes, dislikes, and feelings. Often close friends can provide a new perspective on what makes those we love "tick."

EXPLORING THE ISSUES
---

1. Define "active commitment" in your own words.

2. Would you say that, overall, your parents demonstrated an active commitment to blessing you? Why or why not?

3. In Proverbs 31:10-31, we're introduced to a woman who blesses her family every day. Read that passage and answer the following questions.

a. What things does this woman do to demonstrate an active commitment to her family?

b. How is she viewed by her family?

4. a. Has God been a personal encourager to you? If so, how?

b. If not, why not?

5. Try to recall the first time you were disciplined and you realized it was done for your own good. What did the disciplinarian do that lovingly communicated that?

6. The opening excerpt in this session contains the suggestion that you be lovingly persistent in communicating with someone you want to know better. What guidelines should be followed in trying to communicate with someone who seems unwilling?

7. a. List as many examples as you can of "sharing activities" that provide good opportunities for getting to know another person.

b. What kinds of activities are often shared but *don't* help us know others better?

8. Ask the following questions of the person(s) you would most like to bless through your active commitment.

a. What do you most often daydream about?

b. When you think of the rest of your life, what would you really enjoy doing?

c. Of all the people in the Bible you have studied, who would you most want to be like, and why?

d. What do you believe God wants you to do for His Kingdom?

e. What type of person do you enjoy being around, and why?

f. What's the best part of your day, and what's the worst?

BRINGING IT HOME

1. Having looked now at all five elements of the blessing, think of those people you need to bless. How committed are you to blessing them? As you consider these questions in prayer, ask God to truly make this the first day of the rest of your life in blessing those nearest you.

2. What one person, more than any other, needs to sense your active commitment to bless him or her right now? Plan two or three things you can do in the next week to demonstrate your commitment.

3. In preparation for the next session, think of someone you know well who seems *not* to have received his or her parents' blessing (perhaps yourself). What was the nature of the denial? For example, was the blessing tied to unreachable expectations?

TAKING IT FURTHER
---

1. Read chapter 7 in *The Blessing*.
2. Read the following quotations, and answer the questions after each.

    a. "Promises may get friends, but it is performance that keeps them." (Owen Feltham)
    ▶Think of someone you know who has a habit of breaking promises. How would you characterize his or her relationships with others?
    b. "Example is not the main thing in influencing others. It is the only thing." (Albert Schweitzer)
    ▶How many people come readily to mind who have demonstrated an active commitment to you? How many come to mind who have *not*?
    ▶What kind of commitment do you tend to display to people today?
    ▶What connection do you see between your commitment to others and the type of commitment you have been shown?
    c. "Regret is an appalling waste of energy; you can't build on it; it's only good for wallowing in." (Katherine Mansfield)
    ▶Think of a time you were stalled in taking positive action because of regrets. What are some ways to get going again?

HOMES THAT WITHHOLD
THE BLESSING

IDENTIFYING THE ISSUES

Few people see themselves as struggling with missing out on their family's blessing, but people around them see it. Whether it is reflected in an underlying sense of insecurity, or, more blatantly obvious, in an angry, hostile spirit, we can hide very little from those who know us well. . . .

. . . [We] want to introduce you to the five most common homes we see in counseling that withhold the blessing.

We recognize that there may be more homes than these; but in counseling couples and individuals all over the country, these five patterns have continued to surface time and again. . . .

Our aim . . . is to inspire compassion, not heap criticism on horrible parents. Most horrible parents are people who truly love their children (even if they do not know how to show it) and have tried their best with the information they had. . . .

The First Home: Facing a Flood or a Drought. . . .

. . . One child, for what can be a number of reasons, will be drenched with lush showers of blessing from his or her parents. As a result, outwardly this child thrives and grows.

Unfortunately, sitting "just east" of him or her at the dinner table can be one or more siblings whose emotional lives are like parched ground. So few drops of blessing have fallen on the soil of their lives that emotional cracks begin to form. . . .

The Second Home: Where the Blessing Is Placed Just Out of Reach. . . .

Craig wanted his father's blessing so badly that he had studied diligently to be an A student, just like his father. And receiving his first B meant more to him than losing a perfect grade point. That B meant losing any chance at his father's blessing. This "failure" discouraged Craig so badly that the future was not worth facing. . . .

The Third Home: Where the Blessing Is Exchanged for a Burden. . . .

In this third home that withholds the blessing, a terrible transaction takes place. A child is coaxed by guilt or fear into giving up all rights to his or her goals and desires. In return, the child gets a blessing that lasts only until the parent's next selfish desire beckons to be met. . . .

[The Fourth Home: Where the Blessing Is Ruled by Unyielding Traditions] . . . .

. . . Jim had a role he was expected to fulfill in his family, and Jim had decided it was a mold he did not fit. Such an attitude is an unpardonable sin in homes that fly the banner, "Unyielding Traditions Live Here." In this home the blessing is only given when these traditions are met. . . .

The Fifth Home: Receiving Only a Part of the Blessing.

In this final home, a child does receive the blessing, but only in part. There are several ways in which this can happen, and each has the power to leave a child feeling only half-blessed. . . . [T]hree common situations where a part of the blessing can be withheld [are] divorce, desertion, and adoption.

EXPLORING THE ISSUES

1. Has anyone ever told you that he thought you had

missed out on parental blessing? If so, what did he say? Why do you agree or disagree?

2. a. To help confirm whether you grew up in a home that denied the blessing, rate how closely your childhood home came to each of the five typical blessing-withholding homes. (1 = not at all true of my upbringing; 5 = matches just what I experienced.)

Home #1: Sibling got all the blessing.   1   2   3   4   5

Home #2: Blessing just out of reach.   1   2   3   4   5

Home #3: Blessing exchanged for a burden.
                                         1   2   3   4   5

Home #4: Ruled by unyielding traditions.
                                         1   2   3   4   5

Home #5: Received only a partial blessing.
                                         1   2   3   4   5

b. Find someone you can confide in and tell them why you think you did not receive the blessing.

3. What are some good intentions that go astray and lead parents to withhold their blessing?

4. In Genesis 37:1-11, we see how Joseph was favored by his father above all his brothers. Read that passage and answer the following questions.

> **a.** What happens to the relationship between siblings when one child is favored over the others by one or both of the parents?

> **b.** How can siblings in such a family have a healthy relationship?

5. What steps might you take with your parents to heal the wounds from not having had their blessing?

6. While not receiving parental blessing causes a lot of emotional pain, can you see any good that might come out of it in a person's life—for example, a high level of accomplishment? (Read Genesis 50:15-21 and Romans 8:28.)

1. If this lesson has hit home with you—if you see your childhood home in one of the five typical homes discussed here—what are your feelings now toward your parents? Toward your siblings? Face those feelings honestly. Write them down and read aloud what you wrote.

2. If your feelings toward family members include any negative emotions like anger or bitterness, begin to pray for healing of the hurt and restoration of the relationship. Remember that if the person(s) who hurt you is still alive, there's hope yet that you can receive the blessing. Talk with your parents and siblings about how you feel.

3. In preparation for the next session, go back to suggestion 1 on page 56 to refresh your memory about the many ways God blesses us.

1. Read chapters 8 and 9 in *The Blessing*.
2. Read the following quotations, and answer the questions after each.
    a. "All sorrow and suffering are designed to teach us lessons we would not or could not learn in any other way." (Max Heindel)
    ▶If you have suffered from the lack of a blessing, what helpful lessons have you learned because of it?
    ▶Do you think you could have learned those lessons in any other way? Why or why not?
    b. "Without forgiveness life is governed by . . . an endless cycle of resentment and retaliation." (Roberto Assagioli)
    ▶Who is hurt most when an injured person refuses to forgive his or her offender? Why?
    ▶Who is helped most when he or she chooses *to* forgive? Why?

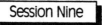

LEARNING TO LIVE
APART FROM THE BLESSING

IDENTIFYING THE ISSUES

We see this . . . twofold tendency in person after person who has missed out on his or her parents' blessing. Many will try to explain away and put off admitting the obvious in their lives. Drawing imaginary pictures of their past or denying the real problems that exist can often keep them from honestly facing their past and their parents. By protecting themselves or their parents, they effectively prevent a cure.

If we never face the fact that we missed out on the blessing, we can postpone dealing with the pain of the past, but we can never avoid it. The legitimate pain of honestly dealing with this situation is what leads to healing and life. When we try to avoid this legitimate pain, we are actually laying on top of it layers of illegitimate pain. . . .

Many of us need to turn on truth's searchlight and shine it on our past. Only then can we be free to walk confidently into the future. . . .

The next recommendation we make to anyone who has missed out on his or her family's blessing is to understand as much as they can about their parents' background. Following this one bit of advice can free many people from wondering why they never received the blessing. . . .

. . . Here is a principle that we hope people who have missed out on the blessing will "tattoo on their brains": In the vast majority of cases, parents who do not give the blessing never received it themselves. . . .

Some children will never, in this life, hear words of love or acceptance from their parents. . . . Some will try to break down the door to their parents' hearts to receive this missing blessing, but all too often their attempt fails. For whatever reason, they have to face the fact that their blessing will have to come from another source. . . .

. . . [When] we accept Christ, we gain not only a secure relationship with our heavenly Father, but we join an entire family of brothers and sisters in Christ! Men and women "with skin on" who can hug us and hold us and communicate God's love, wisdom, and blessing to us! . . .

. . . With a personal relationship with a heavenly Father that is secure, and through a spiritual family that can offer warmth, love, and acceptance, every element of the blessing can be ours and overflowing.

Greg was five when twin sisters came into his family. Although his parents loved him deeply, he grew up feeling that their blessing for him was lessened after the arrival of the twins. Years later, Greg attended one of our seminars in which the blessing was explained. He realized what he had been feeling and determined to talk openly to his parents about it, no matter how difficult it might be.

As he explained his feelings, his mother began to cry, saying she had always feared he felt that way, but she had never known how to talk about it. When his sisters also joined the discussion, the whole family experienced tremendous healing and reaffirmation of their love for one another—all because Greg had the courage to face his past honestly.

Andrea grew up feeling a lack of blessing from her father because he always seemed so distant to her. Although he was cordial, apart from an occasional hug, he had never demonstrated any of the elements of the blessing as far as she could remember. As a young adult, she heard about the concept of the blessing and took the first opportunity to share her feelings with her father.

For the first time, her father explained his background in some detail. He was born in England to parents of minor nobility, and they had raised him in the usual way for their class. Much of his day-to-day care was provided by a nanny, and his relationship with his parents was stiffly formal so as to teach him discipline and proper manners. For example, he always addressed his father as "Sir," never "Daddy," even as a small boy.

Much to Andrea's surprise, she learned that her father felt that, compared to his own parents, he had been a fanatic in trying to give his children the blessing! That discovery gave Andrea a new perspective on her father and how much he truly loved her.

EXPLORING THE ISSUES

1. How does the refusal to face the past honestly affect daily living?

2. To help you face not having received the blessing, complete each of the following sentences as candidly as you can.

a. The most difficult part of talking with my parents about their lack of blessing is . . .

b. When I think about that, it creates feelings of . . .

c. When someone else brings up this subject, I usually . . .

d. I'm afraid that if I faced this honestly the result would be . . .

e. On the other hand, the best thing that could happen is . . .

f. If the people who know me learned about this today, they would probably . . .

g. The most helpful thing someone could do for me in this area is . . .

3. What do you know about how completely your parents were blessed by their own parents?

4. If you have children, how does their perception of how well you were blessed by your parents compare to your perception?

5. If you have children, does their perception of how completely *they* are blessed by *you* match yours? How do you know?

6. What are some of the circumstances that can make it impossible to receive parental blessing?

7. What can we do to help a person who for some reason has no hope of receiving parental blessing?

BRINGING IT HOME
---

1. Do you, like Greg, have some nagging doubt about your parents' blessing? If so, plan some time in the next couple of months when you can discuss it openly with them. Think through ahead of time what you'll say so that you can focus on your feelings rather than accuse them of negligence.

2. If for some reason it's now impossible for you to receive parental blessing, ask God to help you find other Christians who can help to fill the need in your life.

3. In preparation for the next session, list some ways in which your spouse and friends have blessed you. Thank God for those blessings.

TAKING IT FURTHER
---

1. Read chapter 10 in *The Blessing*.

2. Read the following quotations, then answer the questions after them.

    a. "In human relations, kindness and lies are worth a thousand truths." (Graham Greene)

    ▶ This quotation suggests that in dealing with others, it's often better to say what they want to hear rather than the blunt truth. Do you agree or disagree? Why?

    ▶ What is our responsibility when it comes to helping others face their pasts honestly? (Read Proverbs 27:6.)

    b. "Nothing is so soothing to our self-esteem as to find our bad traits in our forebears. It seems to absolve us." (Van Wyck Brooks)

    ▶ How should we respond to the fact that we've acquired certain faults of our parents by imitation?

    ▶ Does admitting we have these faults constitute an indictment of our parents? Why or why not?

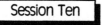

GIVING THE BLESSING TO YOUR SPOUSE AND FRIENDS

IDENTIFYING THE ISSUES

... The elements of the blessing are not just limited to the parent/child relationship. We feel strongly that they can be found at the heart of *any* healthy relationship. ...

Being a Source of Blessing to Your Spouse ....
 The same need for meaningful touching we saw with our children is equally important in a marriage. ...
 Sexual touching is important in any growing relationship; however, it should not be the only time a couple touches. ... [G]enuine intimacy is developed in the small acts of touching in the kitchen, or walking through a mall together hand in hand, or sitting close together on the sofa watching television. ...
 An everyday dose of praise, whether in the form of a word picture or just a statement like "Great dinner, Honey" or "You are so kind to other people" or even "You make me so proud the way you handle the children" can do wonders in a relationship. ...
 While we have talked exclusively about using word pictures to praise a husband or wife, they can also be used to help discuss an important issue or avoid a heated argument.

77

By using a word picture to convey a concern we have, instead of lashing out with damaging words, we can often motivate our mate to change and get across a message we can't seem to get across with only words.

One woman at a conference Gary was leading had a concern she had unsuccessfully tried to communicate to her husband for years. Yet by using a single word picture, she so affected him that he was willing to write her a $150,000 check right on the spot to build her dream house! . . .

Whether it is the fear of entertaining, the need to go on a diet, failing to discipline the children promptly, or keeping a messy house, we do not motivate our mate to change by picturing a negative future. Our mate needs to hear words that picture a special future in the same way our children do, positive words that provide our spouse the room to become all that God can help him or her to become. . . .

Every husband and wife will drop the ball and prove themselves fallible time and again. If we are to be people of blessing, our commitment will rest on our decision to love our spouse "in spite of." Our love must be the kind of love that motivated our heavenly Father to bless us with His Son, in spite of the fact we didn't deserve it and because He knew we needed that blessing so much in our lives. . . .

Being a Source of Blessing to Your Friends.

We constantly meet people who "wish they had a close friend." Many of those same people would not have to make that comment if they knew how to be a "close friend." We discovered in studying the blessing in the Scriptures that an important part of becoming a close friend is to apply each element of the blessing in a friendship.

Glenn was Larry's boss, and he maintained a strict "professional" distance from his employees. When his son was arrested for selling drugs, however, Glenn had no one to lean on for emotional support. Sensing his boss's distress but not knowing the reason behind it, Larry risked offering to talk with Glenn if he felt the need for it. For a few days Glenn said nothing, but then he asked Larry if they could meet for breakfast during the next week.

At first Larry just did a lot of listening as Glenn poured

out his pain. As time went on, Larry was able to give Glenn all the elements of the blessing—a handshake or pat on the back; words of praise for Glenn's positive traits; the hope that God was at work even when circumstances seemed bleak. By modeling these aspects of the blessing over a period of months, Larry showed himself to be a true friend and an enormous help.

EXPLORING THE ISSUES

1. How does giving the blessing to your spouse differ from giving it to your children?

2. How does blessing friends differ from blessing a spouse or a child?

3. What are some ways you've been blessed by your spouse or friends?

4. First Samuel 18:3-4 and 20:41-42 shows us a little of the friendship between David and Jonathan, the son of King Saul. Read those verses, and then answer the following questions:

a. What elements of the blessing did Jonathan give his friend David?

b. How did David respond?

c. What are some other biblical friendships that demonstrate the blessing clearly?

5. What are some specific, practical ways

▶to bless a spouse?

▶to bless friends?

6. Below are six questions for you to answer. They address practical aspects of blessing a spouse or friend. Responding honestly will help you determine how well you bless others.

a. I give my spouse at least five meaningful touches each day. ___ yes ___ no

b. I've praised some character trait of my spouse or close friends in the last week. ___ yes ___ no

c. I've pictured a special future for a friend in the last month. ___ yes ___ no

d. If I passed up a chance to criticize some fault of my spouse or best friend, he or she would probably faint.

___ yes ___ no

e. My spouse and close friends know I'm committed to helping them develop their potential. ___ yes ___ no

f. My friends feel better about themselves after having been with me. ___ yes ___ no

7. a. What's the area of greatest undeveloped potential that you see in your spouse or best friend?

b. How can you encourage him or her to develop that potential without appearing to criticize?

8. Practically speaking, how do we love a spouse or friend "in spite of"?

9. Suppose you want to tell your spouse or a friend that you wish he or she would be a better listener. What's a word picture you could use to get that message across?

1. Review your list of ways in which your spouse or friends have blessed you. If you have trouble recognizing those blessings, ask God to open your eyes to appreciate even the small blessings you receive.

2. For the next thirty days, make a point of praising your spouse or best friend for something at least once a day. Don't let him or her know you're making a special effort at this. Be sure your praise and compliments are genuine, and that you praise traits (such as kindness or loyalty) as well as actions. Note what difference your words of praise make in the relationship.

3. In preparation for the next session, think through some ways in which each of the five elements of the blessing might be applied to your parents.

1. Read chapter 11 in *The Blessing*.
2. Read the following quotations, and then answer the questions.
   a. "Often the difference between a successful marriage and a mediocre one consists of leaving about three or four things a day unsaid." (Harlan Miller)
   ▶Do you agree or disagree with this statement? Why?
   ▶What kinds of things might best be left unsaid between husband and wife?
   ▶What criteria should you follow in deciding?
   b. "There are not many things in life so beautiful as true friendship, and there are not many things more uncommon." (Megiddo Message)
   ▶Why are strong friendships uncommon?
   ▶How many close friendships is it possible to have?
   ▶What qualities do you look for in a friend?
   ▶What qualities do you believe you offer to your friends?
   ▶Read 1 Samuel 18-20, 30:1-6, and 2 Samuel 1:23-26.
   Analyze the elements of true friendship in these pas-

sages and make a commitment to incorporate them in your relationships.

c. "A valuable friend is one who'll tell you what you should be told, even if it offends you." (Frank A. Clark)

▶Does being a true friend ever require putting the friendship at risk? If so, how?

▶Read the following verses to discover the best ways to speak a hard but needed word to a friend:

Proverbs 12:18	Proverbs 25:15,23
Proverbs 16:24	Proverbs 29:20
Proverbs 17:27	Galatians 6:1-2

GIVING THE BLESSING TO YOUR PARENTS

Is it only those . . . who have . . . a hurtful past who need to bless their parents? Certainly not. In fact, the Scriptures direct every child to give the blessing to his or her parents. . . .

When Paul tells us to honor our parents, he is telling us that they are worthy of high value and respect. In modern-day terms, we could call them a heavyweight in our lives! Just the opposite is true if we choose to dishonor our parents.

Some people treat their parents as if they are a layer of dust on a table. . . . Dust is a nuisance and an eyesore that clouds any real beauty the table might have. Paul tells us that such an attitude should not be a part of how any child views his or her parents. . . .

. . . [P]hysicians and researchers are finding out more and more . . . that a close link exists between what we think and how we physically react.

. . . Positive attitudes have been linked with positive physiological changes while negative attitudes can open the door for illness or disease. When persons choose to hate or dishonor their parents because of anger, bitterness, or resentment, they pay a spiritual, emotional, and physical price. . . .

. . . It is common for a parent to think back in guilt on the past. The things that often seem to stand out to parents are not the many positive things they did, but the times they spoke out in anger or did something that accidentally hurt their child. When you bless your parents with words that *attach high value* to them, you can be a tremendous encouragement in their lives. You do not have to pretend a wrong was never committed, but you can forgive them and keep them from self-pity. . . .

. . . [F]or many parents the reason they can only look back to times past is because they do not feel a sense of a future in their lives. You can point out useful and beneficial aspects to your parents' lives, even if those useful qualities are different than when they were younger. . . .

. . . [W]e know that some readers' parents have already died. What about them? What happens when you can't talk face to face with your parents and speak words of blessing to them? . . .

If this is your situation, let us make a few suggestions. First, try writing a letter to that person describing what you would share with him or her if she or he were with you in person. If writing is difficult, make a cassette tape that you can play back and listen to. Remember we are called to honor our parents, not tear up their memory with hateful words. You can still be painfully honest, and yet not sin with your words.

Helen was a young woman who learned she needed to bless her alcoholic father. He had abused her physically while she was growing up, and as soon as she was old enough to leave home, she packed up and moved out. After her parents divorced while she was in college, she had no reason ever to see him again.

Later, however, a co-worker named Karen led Helen to Christ, and she found much of the blessing she needed in her spiritual family at church. But as she grew in her Christian life, she found that certain areas, such as her temper, remained beyond control. She thought for a long time that this showed a lack of faith or of knowledge of the Bible. Then one day, as she looked honestly at her life, she realized that neither of those things was the problem. Instead, she was unwilling to honor her father as God commands. She was held captive by her bitterness toward him, and she was actually becoming more and more like him.

Helen tried to deny the growing conviction that she needed to resolve her feelings toward her dad, but eventually, with the help of her pastor and friends, she arranged to go see him. There she told him about becoming a Christian, and she admitted the hatred she had felt for years. Finally, she asked for his forgiveness. In tears, he asked for her forgiveness as well. And when Helen left her father's house that day, she was finally free of the past, free to enjoy the present and grow into a limitless future.

EXPLORING THE ISSUES
---

1. In your own words, state how each of the five elements of the blessing applies to blessing your parents.

2. In Ephesians 6:1-3, Paul gives us God's command regarding our parents. Read those verses, and then answer these questions:

    a. In what ways can adult children honor their parents?

b. In the context of Exodus 20:12, the promise of long life on the earth (or more accurately, "your days may be long upon the land") refers to the continuation of God's promised blessings. In what ways might God withdraw His blessing if we dishonor our parents? (Read John 14:21 and 15:14.)

c. What choice should we make if doing what we think is right would mean refusing to honor our parents' wishes?

3. What are some of the common ways that people dishonor their parents?

4. If your relationship with a parent isn't good, how, practically, do you honor that parent?

5. a. What mistakes in rearing you might your parents feel guilty about?

b. Have you expressed your forgiveness and restored the relationship?

6. a. Is your parents' outlook on the future generally positive or negative? Why?

b. If it is negative, what can you do to change that?

7. What are some strengths and beneficial aspects of your parents' lives that you can point out to them, especially when they're discouraged?

8. What insights do the following verses offer for honoring elderly parents who can't care for themselves physically or financially?

Genesis 45:1-11

Proverbs 23:22

Proverbs 28:24

Mark 7:11-12

2 Corinthians 12:14

9. If they were asked, would your parents say you demonstrate an active commitment to blessing them? Why or why not?

10. To help you gauge how well you're giving each element of the blessing to your parents, use the five continuums below. If you feel you're not conveying an element very well, put a mark toward the left (non-blessing) side of the continuum. If you *are* conveying that element well, put your mark toward the right (blessing) side of the scale. As you do so, keep the sobering words of Proverbs 30:11 in mind.

Little meaningful touch	Lots of meaningful touch

Few spoken blessings	Many spoken blessings

Express low value	Express high value

Picture a dim future	Picture a special future

Weak commitment	Strong, active commitment

BRINGING IT HOME

1. If you realize you haven't been blessing your parents, ask God for forgiveness and the wisdom and love to begin obeying His commandment.

2. Plan three things you can do in the next month to bless your parents, even if you can't contact them. Try to make these things you're not already doing.

3. In preparation for the next session, list some ways in which a church family is like a natural family and other ways in which it's different.

---

1. Read chapter 13 in *The Blessing*.
2. Read the following quotations, then answer the questions after each.

a. "How sharper than a serpent's tooth it is to have a thankless child." (William Shakespeare)
▶ For what are you most thankful about your parents?
▶ How often and how clearly have you expressed your thanks to them?

b. "I consider that the old have gone before us along a road which we must all travel in our turn, and it is good we should ask them of the nature of that road, whether it be rough and difficult or easy and smooth." (Plato)
▶ What valuable lessons about life have your parents taught you?
▶ What other questions would you like to ask them?
▶ Have you learned more from their words or their example? Why?

c. "In the central place of every heart there is a recording chamber. So long as it receives a message of beauty, hope, cheer, and courage—so long are you young. When the wires are all down and your heart is covered with the snow of pessimism and the ice of cynicism, then, and only then, are you grown old." (Douglas MacArthur)
▶ By this definition, are your parents young or old? Why?
▶ If they're growing old, what can be done to reverse this "aging process"?

A CHURCH
THAT GIVES THE BLESSING

. . . [M]any churches today . . . talk about the blessings of genuine fellowship . . . in a sermon or in a Sunday school class, but do not practice it with people within the church. While we may not like to admit it in the evangelical community, many people who come to our churches find more of the elements of the blessing in a bowling alley than they do inside the church walls.

Instead of letting this discourage those of us inside the church, it should encourage us to learn how to be a people of blessing. We need to learn how to make significant relationships within the church, not superficial ones. . . .

Introducing people to Jesus Christ is the first and foremost way a church can bless others. When men and women are introduced to the Source of blessing, they come face to face with Someone who can be their best friend and their very source of life. . . .

People outside the church will never care how much we know about Christ until they know how much we care for each other. When a body of believers becomes committed to loving each other, then they can truly be called a church that is serious about winning others to Christ. . . .

If Jesus commanded us to be people who deeply love each other, why do so many churches struggle with being warm and sensitive to the needs of others? Is it a lack of loving people in the church?

We fully believe that it is not the lack of caring believers in the church that results in people . . . going away unblessed. Rather, these people lack the knowledge about how they can practically meet the relational needs other people have once they come to know Christ. . . .

Imagine what would happen if an entire church decided to bless those in their fellowship and were trained how to do it! We would have a church where relationship needs were actively being met by a welcoming handshake or hug (meaningful touch); where appreciation for a fine sermon, working in the children's department, or simply listening to a hurting brother or sister was verbally acknowledged (spoken message). We would have groups of believers who acknowledged every member's true worth (attaching high value) and who gave them words of hope and encouragement to reach their God-given potential (a special future). All these elements would be wrapped in the willingness to let people fail and not let them walk away unnoticed, because a decision had been made already that they were valuable (an active commitment).

Unfortunately, Jim did not find the blessing in his church. A mechanic with a failing marriage and a drinking problem, he found the camaraderie he needed with his drinking buddies on the bowling team. Jim was eventually won to Christ, however, by Ed, a fellow mechanic. Jim and his wife then began to attend a fairly large church near their home.

Although they enjoyed the pastor's sermons, they found no one interested in making them feel at home when the services were over. In search of fellowship, they tried a Sunday school class for a few months, but they didn't know people any better at the end of that time than they had at the beginning. And when they dropped out, no one seemed to notice.

Then Ed moved out of state, devastating Jim. Feeling lonelier and lonelier, he eventually drifted out of church and back to the bowling alley and his drinking buddies. This story has no happy ending, and there are many new believers who could tell sadly similar tales.

EXPLORING THE ISSUES
---

1. How well does your church provide the blessing to its people? What are the reasons?

2. What could a church do to help meet the relationship needs of a person like Jim?

3. Is the degree to which a church gives people the blessing just a part of the church's nature—something it does or doesn't have—or is it the result of a deliberate choice on the part of the members? Explain.

(Read the following verses before you answer this question. Pay attention to whether the verses include commands, requests, or statements. Philippians 2:1-4, Colossians 3:12-17, Hebrews 10:24-25.)

4. In Galatians 6:2, we're instructed to "bear one another's burdens." What does that mean in daily living? List some practical ways to do so for members in your church.

5. Jesus gave His followers a command in John 13:34-35, saying our obedience would mark us as His disciples. Read that passage and answer the following questions.

a. Do you agree that Christians need to be committed to loving each other in order for nonbelievers to be won to Christ? Why or why not?

b. What does it mean to be a disciple of Jesus? (Read Mark 8:34-38 and Luke 9:23 and 14:25-35.)

c. What's the best example you've seen of a church providing the blessing to someone who needed it?

6. a. What part of the blessing is it most difficult for a church to provide? Why?

b. How can the difficulty be overcome?

7. a. What are some of the problems that can develop when a person who missed his parents' blessing seeks it in the church?

b. What are some practical guidelines that can lessen the chance that these problems will develop?

8. The following to-be-completed statements are designed to help you look for models of blessing that already exist in your church, then think through your church's potential for blessing. Finish each statement as completely as possible.

a. The individual who most blesses others in my church is . . .

b. That person makes other feel blessed by . . .

c. The *group* within my church that most blesses others is . . .

d. That group does that by . . .

e. I'd like my church to be known in the community as a church that . . .

f. What people actually say about my church is . . .

g. The biggest obstacle to my church developing its potential as a place of blessing is . . .

BRINGING IT HOME

1. Ask God to show you how you can begin to make your church more of a place of blessing in those areas where it falls short of the ideal. Thank Him for the ways in which it already blesses people.

2. Plan a first step you can take in the next month to make your church a greater place of blessing, either on your own or by enlisting the help of others.

TAKING IT FURTHER

1. Read chapter 12 in *The Blessing*.
2. Read the following quotations and answer the questions that follow.
    a. "The church does the most for the world when the church is least like the world." (Warren Wiersbe)
    ▶In what ways does the church need to be different from the world in order to be a place of blessing?
    ▶Are there any ways in which it might bless better by being *more like* the world?

b. "In Galatians we are commanded to bear one another's burdens; instead, we often increase each other's burdens by making each other feel guilty for their pain or anguish." (Ron Lee Davis)

▶Why do we tend to add to—rather than lift—one another's burdens?

▶What effect does this have on the church?

▶What effect does it have on our witness to the world?

c. "One of the prayers I pray as I sit in quiet on Sunday morning preparing for church is, *Lord, who is there you want me to minister to this day?*" (Karen Mains)

▶How sensitive are you to the needs of others?

▶How can you improve your sensitivity?

▶Who can you reach out to and bless *today*?

ENDNOTES

SESSION ONE
Opening quotation from *The Blessing* by Gary Smalley and
John Trent, pages 9, 14, 18-19. Reprinted by permission of
Thomas Nelson Publishers (Nashville, Tenn.). Copyright
© 1987 by Gary Smalley and John Trent.

SESSION TWO
Opening quotation from *The Blessing*, pages 23-28.

SESSION THREE
Opening quotation from *The Blessing*, pages 35-36, 38, 41-44.

SESSION FOUR
Opening quotation from *The Blessing*, pages 49-50, 52, 59,
62-63.

SESSION FIVE
Opening quotation from *The Blessing*, pages 67, 70, 73-74,
76-77, 79.
    1. *The Blessing*, page 80.
    2. For a more detailed explanation of word pictures, see
our book, *The Language of Love.*
    3. See *The Language of Love.*

SESSION SIX
Opening quotation from *The Blessing*, pages 81-82, 89-90, 92-94.

SESSION SEVEN
Opening quotation from *The Blessing*, pages 99-102, 104-108, 111.

SESSION EIGHT
Opening quotation from *The Blessing*, pages 117-120, 123-124, 128, 131, 137.

SESSION NINE
Opening quotation from *The Blessing*, pages 149-151, 153, 158-159, 162.

SESSION TEN
Opening quotation from *The Blessing*, pages 165, 168, 170-172, 176, 179-180.

SESSION ELEVEN
Opening quotation from *The Blessing*, pages 200-201, 203, 205-208.

SESSION TWELVE
Opening quotation from *The Blessing*, pages 188-190, 192-193.

SMALL-GROUP MATERIALS FROM NAVPRESS

BIBLE STUDY SERIES

CRISISPOINTS FOR WOMEN
DESIGN FOR DISCIPLESHIP
GOD IN YOU
GOD'S DESIGN FOR THE FAMILY

LIFECHANGE
LIFESTYLE SMALL GROUP SERIES
QUESTIONS WOMEN ASK
STUDIES IN CHRISTIAN LIVING

TOPICAL BIBLE STUDIES

Becoming a Woman of
    Excellence
Becoming a Woman of
    Freedom
The Blessing Study Guide
Caring Without Wearing
Celebrating Life
Crystal Clear
The Gift of Creation
Growing in Christ

Growing Strong in God's Family
Homemaking
Intimacy with God
Loving Your Husband
Loving Your Wife
A Mother's Legacy
Surviving Life in the Fast Lane
To Run and Not Grow Tired
To Walk and Not Grow Weary
When the Squeeze Is On

BIBLE STUDIES WITH COMPANION BOOKS

Bold Love
From Bondage to Bonding
Hiding from Love
Inside Out
The Practice of Godliness
The Pursuit of Holiness

Secret Longings of the
    Heart
Transforming Grace
Trusting God
The Wounded Heart
Your Work Matters to God

RESOURCES

Curriculum Resource Guide
How to Lead Small Groups
Jesus Cares for Women
The Small Group Leaders
    Training Course

Topical Memory System (KJV/NIV
    and NASB/NKJV)
Topical Memory System: Life
    Issues (KJV/NIV and
    NASB/NKJV)

VIDEO PACKAGES

Abortion
Edge TV
Hope Has Its Reasons
Inside Out

Living Proof
Parenting Adolescents
Unlocking Your Sixth Suitcase
Your Home, A Lighthouse